CW00341366

the call of the forest

AND OTHER POEMS

Other titles by Sangharakshita include

A Survey of Buddhism
A Guide to the Buddhist Path
The Three Jewels
The Religion of Art
The Eternal Legacy
The Rainbow Road *(memoirs)*
Facing Mount Kanchenjunga *(memoirs)*
In the Sign of the Golden Wheel *(memoirs)*
Hercules and the Birds and Other Poems
Complete Poems 1941–1994
In the Realm of the Lotus

SANGHARAKSHITA

the call of the forest

AND OTHER POEMS

WINDHORSE PUBLICATIONS

Published by
Windhorse Publications
11 Park Road
Moseley
Birmingham
B13 8AB

Printed by Interprint Ltd, Marsa, Malta

Cover design Karmabandhu
Cover illustration Photodisc
Design Dhammarati

British Library Cataloguing in Publication Data
A catalogue record for this book is available from the British Library

ISBN 1 899579 24 9

Contents

A Short Biography of Sangharakshita

SANGHARAKSHITA'S first remembered contact with Buddhism is of being held up as a child to inspect a large painting of a Buddha hanging in his grandmother's front hall.

Born Dennis Lingwood in London in 1925, his first opportunity to explore the cultural riches of the world came early, when a suspected heart condition confined him to bed between the ages of eight and ten. Initiated into the culture of East and West by Arthur Mee's *Children's Encyclopaedia*, he went on to pursue a passion for art, literature, and history with great precocity.

At sixteen he discovered through reading the classics of the East that he was a Buddhist. Drafted to

India with the Army in World War Two, he devoted himself as much as possible to the study and practice of the Buddha's teachings.

He stayed in India after the war and was ordained as a monk, and given the name Sangharakshita, which means 'protector of the spiritual community'. It was around this time that he began to experience a tension between his spiritual and his artistic vision which provoked much reflection on the relationship between the Arts and Buddhism.

During the fourteen years he spent in Kalimpong, Sangharakshita continued to read and write prodigiously, his poetry often being inspired by the Himalayan mountains facing his vihara, and by his reflections on the transformative effect of beauty, a theme that runs through much of his writing.

Meanwhile, there was a rising interest in Buddhism in the West. In the hope that his experience might help in leading the way forward, Sangharakshita returned to England in 1964. In 1967 he founded a new Buddhist movement based in London.

Sangharakshita has consistently encouraged the poets, painters, and other artists among his disciples to see their art as spiritual practice, and highlighted the importance of engaging with Western culture and art. He has evolved a body of teachings showing that the integration of the Arts into the spiritual life can help the developing individual to achieve a harmonious integration of reason and emotion.

Now Sangharakshita has handed on his responsibilities to his senior disciples, and is focusing on personal contact with people and, of course, on his writing.

Preface

Sangharakshita is known mostly as a Buddhist teacher and the head of an international Buddhist order who has done much to 'translate' the ancient teachings of the Buddha into the language of our time. He is a much-loved spiritual friend to thousands of men and women in various parts of the world. He also happens to be a poet and poetry lover who has read and composed poetry since he was a child.

It was at the age of twelve, on Christmas morning 1937, in a semi-detached council house in South London, that Sangharakshita (then Dennis Lingwood) found among the presents at his bedside a blue-bound copy of John Milton's *Paradise*

Lost. That morning he had 'the greatest poetic experience of my life ... it was that apocalypse of Miltonic sublimity that made me from that day onwards, if not a poet yet at least a modest practitioner of the art of verse'.

Some people – even some Buddhists – might find the idea of a practising Buddhist writing poetry rather strange. Sangharakshita himself, in his early days as a Buddhist monk, underwent an intense spiritual crisis, torn between a Sangharakshita who wanted to meditate, study the Buddhist scriptures, fast, and so on and a Sangharakshita who wanted to write poetry, meet people, and dream. He eventually suceeded in bringing these two aspects of his personality together, but the question remains for some people: what is the relationship between poetry and the spiritual life?

Some might ask this question as they look through the poems in this book. While it is true that some of the poems deal with obviously Buddhist subjects, such as great teachers and deities, many of them are not overtly Buddhist at all. Indeed, even in this small selection of Sangharakshita's recent poetry, one cannot but be struck by the diversity of subjects about which Sangharakshita has been moved to write. You will find in these pages a poem that celebrates the life of Allen Ginsberg, another that meditates on an early painting by Lama Govinda, and yet another that attempts to get inside the mind of a 'Victorian' housewife. There are poems that emerge from a profound contemplation of nature as well as poems that celebrate spiritual vision.

From this range and diversity of Sangharakshita's poetic subjects we get a clue to understanding how we can combine an intense practice of the Buddha's teachings with writing poetry. The clue is found in the word sympathy. Both the Buddhist and the poet need to cultivate this virtue to the highest possible degree.

By sympathy is meant the imaginative identification with what is other than us, be it with other people, nature, or the spiritual ideal. Someone who is serious about practising Buddhism will need to cultivate – from the very beginning of their spiritual quest – a profound sympathy with others that derives from an intense imaginative identification with them. Such a sympathy is the basis for the fundamental Buddhist virtue of loving-kindness. The poet, too, has to develop sympathy in order to write his poems. In order to create, he too has to imaginatively go out of himself into the life around him. How often have the great poets celebrated and even tried to explain this imaginative identification? Expositions of the subject by Coleridge, Keats, and Shelley spring readily to mind.

Sangharakshita is someone who possesses sympathy to a remarkable degree. This explains why such a wide variety of people love and trust him as their spiritual friend – they know that he can sympathize with them. It also explains why he can respond to great poetry and why he is moved to write on such a wide range of subjects. In the end, there is no conflict between the sympathy of a Buddhist and the sympathy of a poet, and it is interesting to note that Sangharakshita has quoted Shelley's famous passage on the imagination in both an exposition of Buddhist ethics and an essay on poetry:

> The great secret of morals is love; or a going out of our own nature, and an identification of ourselves with the beautiful which exists in thought, action, or person, not our own. A man, to be greatly good, must imagine intensely and comprehensively; he must put himself in the place of another and of many others; the pains and pleasures of his species must become his own.

We must also bring sympathy to the way we read poetry. I would recommend that when you read these poems you do what I have done: take them to a quiet corner and read them aloud to yourself. You will notice that they are quite unlike much of today's poetry. They don't come off the page drawing attention to themselves through shocking words, or special effects, or by being shrouded in obscurity. But don't underestimate them. They have a force that derives from the fact that Sangharakshita says what he means in plain and simple language.

It would also be true to say that Sangharakshita offers these poems in a spirit of sympathy. They are poems given in friendship. Sangharakshita makes no great claims for his poetry, but offers them so that people can get to know some of his more intimate moods and inspirations, which he can express only in verse.

As well as sympathy, there is another element that stands out particularly in this collection: the theme of death. Sangharakshita is seventy-five this year, and it is clear that he is beginning to 'live his death'. He is looking death in the eye and looking with that strange combination of confidence and humility for which many of us know him. He looks with a confidence and humility born of his deep faith in the spiritual ideal. As he says in the poem 'Splendor Solis':

Behind the curtain of the dark,
Oh he is there, oh he is there.

Padmavajra
Padmaloka
Norfolk
March 2000

The Call of the Forest

What does the forest whisper
With every wind-stirred leaf,
From many-centuried oak tree
To hour-old blossom-sheaf?
What does the forest whisper
When nightingales are dumb
And cicadas fall silent?
The forest whispers, 'Come'.

What does the forest whisper
In sunshine and in shade,
Down every moss-hung alley,
In each deer-haunted glade?
What does the forest whisper
When full or crescent moon
Steeps nodding crests in silver?
The forest whispers, 'Soon'.

What does the forest whisper
From depths primeval, where
A sound is lost in stillness
As clouds dissolve in air?
What does the forest whisper

When from the darkling bough
Drop one by one the dead leaves?
The forest whispers, 'Now'.

But the whisper's a dream-whisper,
For years on years have flown
Since oak and ash and holly
Could call the land their own.
The whisper's a dream-whisper,
For Cities of the Plain
Usurp the once-green kingdom
Of forests they have slain.

The whisper's a dream-whisper,
For 'forest' is a dream
Of days when Man through Nature
Had sense of a Supreme.
The whisper's a dream-whisper
Of a time when he could feel
In the pressure of the actual
The touch of the Ideal.

The whisper's a dream-whisper,
But dreams are of the Soul
And Soul itself a forest

Beyond the mind's control.
The whisper's a Soul-whisper,
That like a muffled drum
Calls, 'From your mind-built Cities,
O Man, to Freedom come!'

In Memory of Allen Ginsberg

Best minds, he called us, of his generation,
And howled, at our destruction, through the night;
But some of us, thanks to a Word well spoken,
Survived, and deep in darkness saw a light.

Now, Allen, you are gone, best mind of all
For honesty in thought and word and deed,
And I salute you, though I cannot write
My name to every item of your creed.

But let me pluck a leaf from Cowley's book,
And separate the dogma from the dean
In some respects, give praise where praise is due,
And celebrate the *man* that you have been.

Lover of Blake and boys, to you was given
The rage that burns within the tyger's heart,
To you, likewise, the meekness of the lamb,
The victim's posture, but the hero's part.

You were no devil, though some thought you were,
No angel, either, but a star whose spears
Down on the floor of heaven long since were thrown
Gladly; and *earth* was watered by your tears.

God on his throne, if God above there be,
Has surely smiled to hear you sing and play
Your cymbals. Now, as by his side you sit,
He crowns you king of his eternal May.

The Minor Poets

Shakespeare, Milton, Wordsworth, Coleridge
Are godlike spirits; we are men,
And cannot always brook their splendour –
The Minor Poets please us then.

The singers of the lesser vision,
Who never soar beyond our ken –
When we grow tired of greatness, they,
The Minor Poets, soothe us then.

Oppressed by fears, by doubts bewildered,
From Melancholia's cluttered den –
For all their charm, for all their solace,
The Minor Poets, we thank them then.

Faded bindings, dusty edges,
Words underscored by studious pen –
Rejoice to see them on the shelves,
And *praise* the Minor Poets then.

The Angel in the House

I am the Angel in the House
I am the Angel
Virginia Woolf tried to strangle
But I'm still around
I wipe children's noses
Place a cool hand on hot foreheads
Make tea
Knit
Welcome tired husbands home from work
Et cetera
I like doing these things
And I guess I've as much right to exist
As any other kind of Angel
Especially the Female Writing Angel
Who despite having a private income
And a Room of Her Own
And a perfect husband
And two or three lovers
And her own publishing house
Goes and throws herself in the nearest river
(Silly woman)
So as I move about the House
Wings demurely folded

Skirts rustling
I sing this song to myself

    Virginia Woolf
    All teeth and pearls
    Was fond of men
    But fonder of girls

    Virginia wrote
    Pages and pages
    Thought she was heir
    Of all the ages

    Though she was Leslie
    Stephen's daughter
    She ended up
    In three feet of water

Frozen Tulips

Frozen tulips, mauve and green,
You have lost your heavenly sheen,
Transported, from I know not where,
To florists in the city square.

Perhaps, hermetically sealed,
You left by air the happy field
Where millions of you, rainbow-hued,
With scent and colour were imbued.

Now, stiffly in my vase you stand,
Petals unable to expand,
Your green to yellow slowly turning,
And mauve to black, as though from burning.

Splendor Solis
After Omraam Mikhael Aivanhov

Though ninety million miles away,
A ball of heat, and light, and song,
His gifts to us are infinite,
And yet we do him grievous wrong.

We say that he is dead, although
We live. Can life from death arise?
Oh hail him monarch of your hearts,
As sovereign of the azure skies!

That blaze of light unbearable,
That golden splendour, pure and whole,
That burning disc, that crimson orb,
Is temple to a living soul.

So worship him at dawn and dusk,
And noon; at midnight breathe a prayer.
Behind the curtain of the dark,
Oh he is there, oh he is there.

Lama Govinda in Capri

After seeing a reproduction of his painting
'Capri at Night'

Capri at Night. A harmony
In brown and black, with here and there
An orange light that softly falls
On walls cylindrical and bare
Pierced by dark apertures like eyes
And mouths, but barren of replies.

Beyond, an alley, and an arch
That leads into a deeper gloom,
While high above, a yellow light
Shines faintly from an upper room
In which, perhaps, one sick or dying
On an uneasy bed is lying.

Artist and sage, whose poet soul
Served Truth and Beauty all your days,
Did you then have to wander, lost,
Through dark and labyrinthine ways,
Before at last could rise for you
The dome of Kailash, white against the blue?

The Poet

I have never regretted
Buying a book,
Though it left me no money
With which to hook
A woman, or spend
With a like-minded friend.

I have never regretted
Not being rich,
Though nights I had
To lie in the ditch
With a rose overhead
And mud for bed.

I have never regretted
Serving the Muse,
Though well she knew
I could not refuse
The heavenly chore,
Though at death's door.

Mother Goose Revisited
or Innocence and Experience

My Granny said that little girls
Were made of all things nice,
Making particular mention
Of sugar and of spice.

But as for little boys, she said,
It really was heart-breaking,
For frogs and snails and puppy-dogs' tails
All went into *their* making.

But since I was the kind of boy
Who loved the croaking race
I didn't mind what Granny said,
And so was in disgrace.

I had at home a pet green frog
That I loved tenderly,
And liked to think that frogs like him
Were really part of me.

While as for snails, I often wished
(And asked it in my prayers)

That *my* two eyes were mounted
On long thin stalks like theirs.

That *my* two eyes were mounted
On long thin stalks like theirs.

And puppy-dogs? Oh puppy-dogs,
So playful, cute, and small,
I'm sure my very dearest wish
Was to be one, tail and all.

But now I am a big boy
With lessons to repeat,
I've learned that sugar's poisonous,
Although it is so sweet,

While spices, taken in excess,
Are really rather dire;
Red chillies, in particular,
Can set your throat on fire.

So I wonder why my Granny,
As she stroked my golden curls,
Should have given me that nonsense
About little boys and girls.

After Visiting New Zealand

What I am left with
Now the long journey's been made?
A handful of memories
And a polished piece of jade.

Letter to Ananda

Ánanda, thirty years ago
We walked abroad through sleet and snow
Along the Embankment, underneath
A freezing sky. Apollo's wreath
Was yours, Tiresias' fillets mine,
Though you from discontent divine,
Night after night, in coffee bars
Would grasp at novelistic stars
Beyond your early reach; while I,
Fresh from a cloudless Indian sky,
Down in my weekly catacomb
Strove hard to make a little room
In people's minds for faith and hope
Beyond the *Daily Mirror's* scope.
Now three decades and more are flown
And each has reaped as he has sown.
In Bristol you, these many days,
Are crowned with bright poetic bays
(Bays only seen of those, I grant,
Who've signed the Muses' covenant
In Churchill's 'blood, toil, tears and sweat'
Without repining or regret);
While I, in Birmingham, can see
Where once a seed was, now a tree

Beneath whose branches, widely spread,
Thousands are on ambrosia fed
Who once had only stones for bread
(An image from the Bible drawn
Yet common property, like corn).
But poet or prophet, lion or lamb,
In Bristol or in Birmingham,
We face a common destiny:
You're fifty, I am seventy-three,
And do not know how many times
Again we'll hear the ponderous chimes
Of old Big Ben (per courtesy
Of your once boss, the BBC)
Before we stand on Styx's shore
(Not that we really knew before),
There to wait till Charon yields
Us passage to the Elysian Fields;
Or ere (another speculation,
Or glorious imagination)
We somehow wake to find ourselves
On lotus-calices, like elves,
And as the petals open see
The wonders of Sukhávati.
But whether to Elysium,
And heroes' company, we come,
Or whether join, with dance and song,

The noble Bodhisattva-throng,
To feel with them the Buddha's grace
And sense, beyond the Light, his face,
Beneath the jewel-trees, in the Happy Place,
Our time is short. Oh let us strive
To keep the precious link alive
With visits and with messages
From home or from beyond the seas;
And if sometimes we cannot meet
Be sure to keep our friendship sweet
With spices of the written word,
By which the heart is strangely stirred.
Donne's dictum down the ages rolls
Unchallenged: 'Letters mingle Souls.'

Donne's Bell

Jack Donne he was a Roaring Boy
And loved a Southwark wench;
He loved the bottle, loved the Muse,
And dearly loved his friends;
For youth must learn, and so will burn
The candle at both ends.

Dean Donne he was a preacher,
Grandiloquent, severe;
In Paul's church-yard he wrenched his text
Twenty times a year;
For when you're old the blood runs cold
And soon you're on your bier.

When naked at the bar of heaven
John Donne for judgement stands,
Without his sword, without his plume,
Without his cap and bands,
He'll get from God a kindly nod
Because God understands.

He understands that man is clay
As well as breath of heaven,
And that the second's to the first

As one to six or seven,
And that to bake a human cake
There must be dough *and* leaven.

Though which is clay, which heavenly breath,
Men cannot always tell,
And therefore should be slow to think
A soul in heaven or hell.
Come weal or woe, we only know
'It tolls for *thee*,' that bell.

Transmission

'Grain threshed and ready?'
'Ready, long ago.'
'Come then at midnight;
Don't let others know.'

Two heads together
In the Master's room.
Diamond words whispered:
A thousand flowers bloom.

Padmasambhava

Riding a tiger
The Guru came,
Smile fierce and friendly,
Eyes aflame.

Riding a tiger
From coast to coast,
With his vajra he scattered
The demon host.

Guru, great Guru,
Dispel my sin;
Hurl back the demon
Hordes within;

Transform them to powers
That protect the Right –
Thou, the Thousand-armed,
Thou, the Infinite Light.

Revenge

Red were the leaves upon the beech
Between me and the setting sun,
But redder on the turf beneath
The heart's blood of my brother's son.

And that is why at break of day
The sun shall see upon my knife,
And on the castle steps, the blood
Of those who foully took his life.

O he was fair and *she* was fair,
Yet one was fairer, wealthier still,
And so the traitress and her man
Conspired my brother's son to kill.

In shadow of the castle wall
I wait to see the sun uprise,
My hand upon my knife, a mist
Of blood, red blood, before my eyes.

Guhyaloka: July 1998

Back in the magic valley
I breathe the smoke-free air
And listen to the silence
Distilling everywhere.
Far from the roar of traffic,
Far from the frantic crowd,
I feel my soul expanding
With dreams not disallowed.

Back in the verdant valley
The pine trees lift their arms
As if in joyous welcome
To this refuge from all harms; –
To this refuge – or this respite –
From the venom-dripping tongue
And the shafts that fly in darkness
From a bow by malice strung.

Back in the fragrant valley,
Care-emancipate, alone,
I communicate in silence
With the giant shapes of stone –
Grey, ancient forms that tell me,

In the stillness, 'Time will cure.
Meanwhile, be calm, be silent;
The secret is: Endure.

'We endure the cold of winter,
We endure the summer's heat,
Clouds resting on our shoulders,
Trees crouching at our feet;
And even when the storm-gods
In furious cavalcade
Sweep through the darkening heavens
We are no whit dismayed.

'Yea, though the lightning flashes,
Yea, though the thunder rolls,
They cannot move our spirits,
They cannot shake our souls.
Earth-born, no god affrights us,
No younger power defeats;
Wrapped in eternal silence
We keep our ancient seats.'

Back in the secret valley,
I hear their soundless voice;
I hear their admonition;

I hear it, and rejoice.
Though the 'worldly winds' assail me,
Though friends my cause abjure,
Far from the magic valley
The word will be: Endure.

The Pilgrim

'Who is this, in pilgrim garments,
Who kneels before St Peter's throne?'
'Forgive my sins, O Holy Father,
For Venus' secrets I have known.

'Seventeen years upon her mountain
Did I serve the heathen dame,
Learned the arts by Church forbidden
And renounced the Christian name.'

'Not on earth and not in heaven
Can your sins forgiven be;
Sooner will this staff I carry
Bear blossoms like a living tree.'

The pilgrim has from Rome departed,
A third day rises cool and bright;
Pope Urban, waking, sees with wonder
His staff has blossomed in the night.

With news of sins by heaven forgiven
His messengers scour hill and plain;
The pilgrim's not in croft or castle,
Nor was Tannhäuser seen again.

Revised Version
With Apologies to Philip Larkin

They bring you up, your mum and dad.
They don't know how to, but they do.
They buy you things they never had
And save some money, just for you.

For they were brought up in their turn
By folk in Oxfam hats and coats,
Who played at being soft or stern
With laughter bubbling in their throats.

Man hands on happiness to man.
It rises like a coastal shelf.
Get in as early as you can,
And have a lot of kids yourself.

Three Plumes

I understand the blind old king who rode into
    battle
At the head of his troops, a knight on either side
    to guide him.
He did not wait for Death, but went bravely to
    meet him;
The three white plumes on his helmet danced in
    the sunlight.

White Tara

Appearing from the depth of heaven,
The white-robed goddess, calm and bright,
Sheds moon-like on this lower world
The blessing of her silver light.

Seven eyes she has, all open wide,
In face and forehead, hands and feet,
For she of Pure Awareness is
Embodiment and paraclete.

One hand, in teaching gesture raised,
Imparts a wisdom thrice-profound;
The other, open on her knee,
For endless giving is renowned.

A lotus at her shoulder grows,
Complete with flower, and bud, and fruit;
Her form is straight and still, for she
Is grounded on the Absolute.

'Awake! Arise!' she seems to say,
'Leave dreams, leave sloth, leave passions vile!'
Oh may we, seeing her, go forth
Encouraged by her perfect smile.

The Dance of Death

You dance with emperor, pope, and king,
With knight and dame of high degree;
You dance with youth, you dance with eld,
And one day you will dance with me.

You take for partner whom you please;
To choose is yours, and yours alone,
And one day I will surely find
Your bony hand within my own,

Your bony knee against my knee,
As whirling with you in the dance
My eyes behold, an inch away,
Your ghastly, grinning countenance.

But if I do not shrink from it,
And boldly look you through and through,
Your bony frame in dazzling light
Will be dissolved, and born anew.

Oh you a shining angel shape
Will be, and I, released from strife,
Will find the Dance of Death to be
The Revels of Eternal Life.

THE WINDHORSE symbolizes the energy of the enlightened mind carrying the Three Jewels – the Buddha, the Dharma, and the Sangha – to all sentient beings.

Buddhism is one of the fastest-growing spiritual traditions in the Western world. Throughout its 2,500-year history, it has always succeeded in adapting its mode of expression to suit whatever culture it has encountered.

Windhorse Publications aims to continue this tradition as Buddhism comes to the West. Today's Westerners are heirs to the entire Buddhist tradition, free to draw instruction and inspiration from all the many schools and branches. Windhorse publishes works by authors who not only understand the Buddhist tradition but are also familiar with Western culture and the Western mind. Manuscripts welcome.

For orders and catalogues contact

Windhorse Publications
11 Park Road
Birmingham
B13 8AB
UK

Windhorse Books
P O Box 57441
Newtown
NSW 2042
Australia

Weatherhill Inc
Monroe Turnpike
Trumbull
CT 06611
USA

WINDHORSE PUBLICATIONS is an arm of the Friends of the Western Buddhist Order, which has more than sixty centres on five continents. Through these centres, members of the Western Buddhist Order offer regular programmes of events for the general public and for more experienced students. These include meditation classes, public talks, study on Buddhist themes and texts, and 'bodywork' classes such as t'ai chi, yoga, and massage. The FWBO also runs several retreat centres and the Karuna Trust, a fund-raising charity that supports social welfare projects in the slums and villages of India.

Many FWBO centres have residential spiritual communities and ethical businesses associated with them. Arts activities are encouraged too, as is the development of strong bonds of friendship between people who share the same ideals. In this way the FWBO is developing a unique approach to Buddhism, not simply as a set of techniques, less still as an exotic cultural interest, but as a creatively directed way of life for people living in the modern world.

If you would like more information about the FWBO visit the website at www.fwbo.org or write to

London Buddhist Centre
51 Roman Road
London
E2 0HU
UK

Aryaloka
Heartwood Circle
Newmarket
NH 03857
USA

ALSO FROM WINDHORSE

SANGHARAKSHITA
COMPLETE POEMS 1941–1994

Sangharakshita has dedicated himself to helping people transform their lives not only through his work as a Buddhist teacher but also through the medium of verse, for in his poetry he combines the sensitivity of the poet with the vision born of a life of contemplation and uncompromising spiritual practice.

Here we have the opportunity to listen to a unique voice and to be uplifted by the reflections of an extraordinary person and an accomplished teacher.

528 pages, hardback
ISBN 0 904766 70 5
£17.99/$34.95

SIR EDWIN ARNOLD
THE LIGHT OF ASIA

This inspiring poem by Sir Edwin Arnold (1832–1904), though
written more than a hundred years ago, retains the power to move
us in a way that no prose rendering of the life of the Buddha can.
We cannot but admire the courage, determination, and self-sac-
rifice of the Indian prince who, out of compassion, left his palace
to find a remedy for the sufferings of the world.

192 pages, hardback, with glossary
ISBN 1 899579 19 2
£ 9.99/$19.95

STEPHEN PARR (ANANDA)
NORTH OF THE FUTURE

In this comprehensive collection Ananda guides us through the complex webs of love and family relationships, portraying people and places with language that is direct yet far-reaching in its eloquence. These are poems of poignancy and humour, inspired by the Buddhist insights of impermanence and interconnected-ness.

280 pages, hardback
ISBN 0 904766 76 4
£11.99/$23.95

SANGHARAKSHITA

A STREAM OF STARS: REFLECTIONS AND APHORISMS

A Stream of Stars is a collection of aphorisms, poems, and writings by the eminent Western Buddhist teacher, Sangharakshita. Encompassing culture and society, relationships and the human condition, these incisive teachings illuminate many aspects of life.

   With clarity, insight, and flashes of humour, Sangharakshita provokes us to thought and then to aspiration: an aspiration to true happiness and freedom.

136 pages, with photographs
ISBN 1 899579 08 7
£6.99/$13.95

SANGHARAKSHITA

THROUGH BUDDHIST EYES: TRAVEL LETTERS

Throughout his extraordinary life, Sangharakshita has touched
the lives of many thousands of people. After wandering barefoot
across India in search of spiritual teachings, befriending hermits
and lamas, and working among India's most socially deprived
people, he founded a worldwide community of Buddhists.

In these letters he shares what it is like to be Sangharakshita.
He reflects deeply on his experience, and reveals what is in his
mind as he goes about his life in London, Italy, New Zealand,
Wales, the USA, Germany, and Spain.

376 pages
ISBN 1 899579 23 0
£14.99/$29.95